THIS BOOK
BELONGS TO:

_____
Birth date:

_____
Birth time:

_____
Birth location:

_____

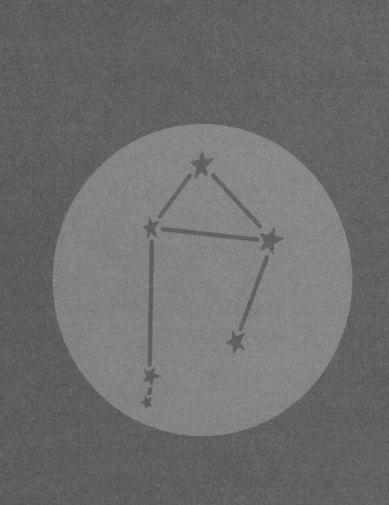

ZODIAC SIGNS

LIBRA

ZODIAC SIGNS

LIBRA

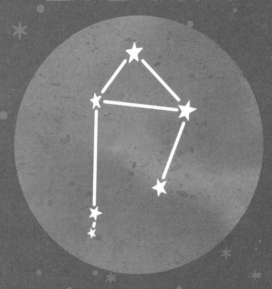

GABRIELLE MORITZ

STERLING ETHOS
New York

STERLING ETHOS
New York

An Imprint of Sterling Publishing Co., Inc.
1166 Avenue of the Americas
New York, NY 10036

ISBN 978-1-4549-3895-8

Distributed in Canada by Sterling Publishing Co., Inc.
c/o Canadian Manda Group, 664 Annette Street
Toronto, Ontario M6S 2C8, Canada
Distributed in the United Kingdom by GMC Distribution Services
Castle Place, 166 High Street, Lewes, East Sussex BN7 1XU, England
Distributed in Australia by NewSouth Books
University of New South Wales, Sydney, NSW 2052, Australia

For information about custom editions, special sales, and premium
and corporate purchases, please contact Sterling Special Sales at
800-805-5489 or specialsales@sterlingpublishing.com.

Manufactured in China

2 4 6 8 10 9 7 5 3 1

sterlingpublishing.com

Cover design by Elizabeth Mihaltse Lindy
Cover and endpaper illustration by Sarah Frances
Interior design by Nancy Singer
Zodiac signs ©wikki33 and macrovector/freepik

CONTENTS

⚖

INTRODUCTION

When it comes to the zodiac, few signs have a sweeter reputation than Libra. And it's not by mistake. The sign of the scales is inherently charming, as Libra strives to be in meaningful connection with all of the world around them. They are the great balancers, easy lovers, and subtle reflectors. To be born with a Libra Sun is to embody beauty, justice, and grace, in all forms. Through the wisdom of the scales, they teach us balance and show us what is fair. And they make it look easy, despite the many responsibilities the role can carry with it.

The world is often quick to oversimplify the nature of Libra, but there are many unseen complexities to this sign. Libras are so much more than pretty. They are so much more than a significant other. And they are so much more than easy and soft. Libra, like all signs, has layers. And to begin to illuminate and peel back some of these layers, we must look at the essential nature and fundamentals of this sign. Before we jump into the life and perspective of a Libra, we must know where they're coming from and why.

By examining Libra's specific set of rulerships and correspondences, we can uncover and define their specific nature. By thoroughly exploring these associations, we can come into a rich understanding. The laundry list to be looked into includes the sign's symbol or archetype, its ruling planet, the sign's element, its modality, its polarity, and also a tarot card. And what may sound technical or confusing from that list you'll soon see to be rather intuitive and informative. As we prepare to discuss Libra's fullness, let's first review their unique correspondences and build a foundational knowledge of what is to be woven throughout this book.

LIBRA'S CORRESPONDENCES

SYMBOL: The Scales—The first layer to peel back, and certainly the most well known, is the sign's symbol: the scales. And just what do scales do? What is their function in the world? In the most basic of definitions, they are an inanimate object comparing the weight of two things. An impartial tool used to illuminate equality, or the lack thereof. It is from the scales that we know Libra as the sign of balance. And it is worth noting that of all the zodiacal symbols, Libra is the only sign to be represented by an object rather than an animal or being. This is an important distinction to the singularity of Libra's character and deeper aims. The scales provide a service, information, judgements, and evaluations. Functioning as a tool, they operate by and for others. Without others, they simply sit—balanced, still, and empty. With this, there is both a coolness and an eagerness in Libran interactions. On their own, Libras are able to rest and recalibrate, two very necessary things, especially for the scales to function at their best. But it is not until they are engaged with other people and ideas that they come to life. And in coming to life, shifting and sharing with and for others, they learn the need for finesse in their relationships so as to preserve their own well-being. In speaking to the Libran experience, the symbol of the scales will come up again and again as a critical reference point.

PLANET: Venus—The next major player for the sign of Libra is the planet Venus. For Libra, it is their planetary ruler. Venus is the planet that governs their nature and essence, informing what they care about most. And Venus being the planet of beauty, sweetness, pleasure, and connection, Libras are naturally drawn to these things. It's thanks to this rulership that Libra has gained the reputation of being such a socialite, sweetheart, aesthete, and flirt. Working with this rulership, the placement of Venus in the birth charts of those born with Libra Suns is incredibly important. Venus placements reveal specific depths and qualities for each Libra. Every Libra Sun would be wise to develop a deeper awareness to their natal Venus, as it profoundly influences their own unique expression of the sign. Due to this relationship, we will look at the nuances that different Venus placements cultivate for Libras in each chapter.

ELEMENT: Air—Of the four astrological elements—fire, earth, air, water—Libra is imbued with the element of air. Just like the signs of Gemini and Aquarius, Libra is gifted with a sharp and active mind. The air element holds the energy of communication, ideas, expression, reason. As an air sign, Libra have direct access to these powers via their wit, logic, language, and lightness. Their inherent airiness seeks to keep them afloat, allows them to think their way through and out of things, and keeps them well connected to the webs of community and information.

MODALITY: Cardinal—Another facet of the zodiac is modality, of which there are three: cardinal, fixed, and mutable. Libra—along with Aries, Cancer, and Capricorn—is a cardinal sign. This component of Libra's expression is one that is initiating and compels the sign to action and fresh starts. Each of the cardinal signs marks the turning of the seasons, the changing of the light. With Libra, we experience equinox energy, a point of balance between day and night, rest and activity—yet another reminder of the sign's affinity to symmetry. Libra encourages us to start again from a neutral point of view, and to initiate new connections that can keep us in balance, hold us in harmony. The spark of inspiration unique to Libra is one that prioritizes and celebrates equality, fairness, and shared resources.

POLARITY: Positive—The last astrological note we will speak to is polarity. The signs are equally divided between positive and negative polarities—alternating every other sign—with the odd-numbered signs expressing the positive polarity and the even-numbered expressing the negative polarity. As the seventh sign of the zodiac, Libra is one of the positive signs, carrying with it an active and expressive charge. They tend toward extroversion, engagement, and activity.

TAROT CARD: Justice XI—Beyond the astrological traits, Libra has ties to the tarot as well. Many connections have been made between astrology and tarot, with each of the twelve signs being linked to a Major Arcana card. For Libra, their corresponding tarot card is that of Justice. Most commonly, its imagery depicts a courtly figure, seated between two pillars, holding an upright sword in one hand—the tool of air—and a scale in the other. It's a visual that epitomizes the values and strengths of Libra.

Having covered the fundamentals of the sign, we can now look to explore various facets of the Libra identity. Remember these threads as the foundation. These keys to the sign will be referenced both directly and indirectly going forward, and they provide the basis for understanding Libra at their core.

LIBRA

as a Child

As we enter the world—small, precious, and new—we each carry with us a particular energy. As children we hold a unique and yet untouched signature of being. We bring with us great potential and promise for who we are to become. And in these early days, we begin to know and to show what it is to be born under a particular Sun.

A Libra child is imbued with a light that is looking to spark balance. The rays that shine upon their emergence, that mark their becoming, are those of the Libra Sun—the season of harmony, togetherness, justice, and connection. Under these skies, the little Libran carries a pure and soft expression. They embody the energy of the scales in a fundamental way, as they are just beginning to become themselves.

There is a simple sweetness to the Libra child. With an eagerness to please and a contagious contentedness, they are likely to be smiling, observing, and engaging from a very early age. Their Venusian nature emits a warmth and kindness that pulls them into connection and teaches them to enjoy what is shared.

Employing the sacred tool of Venus—and the very image of the planet's glyph—Libras act as mirrors. And in their early days, their mirroring is pivotal in helping them learn how to be. Trying on the behaviors they see teaches them a great deal, and in this way, they are very attuned and responsive children. They pick up on surrounding energies—from parents, siblings, caretakers, pets—and they amplify their experience in their reflection of things.

When good things surround the Libra child, it feels lovely. They are able to magnify the warm energy they thrive in, as it lifts their energy and emanates outward. But when things are difficult, the young Libra can sometimes over-inflate perceived angst. When they cannot soothe a room or a problem, they are unsettled by the reality of their discomfort. These children often don't understand why they can't feel better or why someone can't be happier.

Sometimes this discomfort leads them to shut down emotionally or look for a place to project their experience. For this reason, it is vital that Libra children are taught early on to name and to know their emotional experience and how it is separate and different from those of the people they are in relationship with. It is easy for this child to prioritize others' feelings or to disassociate from their own. Their airy nature can quickly come in to sweep them off their feet when they don't like the way their lived reality feels.

Soothing a troubled young Libra is often as simple as sharing time with them and their imagination. Cultivate ease, play, and language around their fantasies, while also holding space for their felt experiences. Teach them that these experiences are just as valuable as their sweeter hopes and visions. And strive to keep their container as soft as possible. For these babes, it can be quite difficult to deal with unstable people or places. They don't yet have the ability or awareness to change or understand crunchy circumstances, so they look to the others in their lives to help ease the way.

And those others are their way! Friends, babysitters, coaches, relatives—as many bonds as they're open to. A diversity of relationships is important for expanding this child's understanding of themselves and who they can be. As they try on the traits of their partners, they are seeking out traits of their own. This is why a rich community is so important, so that they don't over-identify with behaviors that aren't true to them. It is natural for them to have an adaptable personality, but without early exposure to different types of people, it can be hard for a Libra to know what is unique and authentic about themselves in later years.

Even in stories, movies, and shows, presenting them with many characters, layered perspectives, and varied experiences will help to keep their minds open. And for the timid or shy Libra child, such exposure can help them learn about people in a manageable way. These kids should never be pushed into relationships or socializing that they are not wanting or ready for. Human connection is something they must be allowed to come to on their own terms, as it is so vital to their identity. It is important that relationships be something they are able to trust.

And beyond the social aspects, sometimes they simply need to witness other people to better note their own skills and persona. When they stand back and observe, they are able to collect valuable information that enhances their ability to decipher and discern the world around them. They are learning how people work to learn how life works, and they are developing a sensitivity to patterns and connections at large.

Finding these common threads often comes with ease for Libra kiddos, and it can be encouraged in fun and simple ways. Word games, puzzles, checkers, cards—play that encourages them to notice symmetries, similarities, and differences, and that asks for a strategy, will see them shine. And charades, dolls, figurines, and playtime are also realms in which these kids get to try on new personalities. They can provide opportunities for these kids to safely and gently process their experiences. A Libra child may feel better able to express their difficult or unpleasant emotions through the guise of a toy or a puppet, or maybe even an imaginary friend. What they may not be ready to identify as their own, or what they may find less than lovable, they can release and witness through a projected self.

Additionally, this mirroring and reflecting can show up quite literally. There is a real fascination with seeing things another way. Water, mirrors, windows, glitter, photographs. Seeing and being seen from another perspective is really compelling for them. Things can be the same but different, viewing the experience of another, witnessing all of the many sides—along with just being able to see themselves in a new way.

Another layer of the mirror, of their Venusian way, is beauty. There is a real love and draw to images. Both images of self and images of the world, they all have the potential to be made beautiful, to radiate with pleasure and pleasantness. A Libra child will have an eye for such a glow. For some, it might result from watching a parent put on makeup and get ready in the morning, and then wanting to do the same for themselves or their favorite dolls. It might mean they want their room to look a certain way. Maybe they loved a specific coloring book and need their palette to fit a certain style. Aesthetics are inherently dear to them and can be expressed in any number of ways. Noting and indulging their interest will help them feel seen and appreciated, calm and at peace, as well as immersed in an amusing and attractive space.

At this early stage of life, finding regularly peaceful environments helps Libras to feel stable and secure. And another way little Libras reach for this is in asking for fairness. These kids come here with a preexisting notion of equality and of what is right. Ultimately, they are working to cultivate justice in the world, but before they are able to navigate the full complexities of this, they start with naming what is fair.

There may be a fixation on what they believe fair is, freely proclaiming its virtues or questioning its presence in the actions of others. "That's not fair" can become a real catchphrase in the face of disappointments or disparity. Equal distribution of resources, the ability to share with others, and being a nice person are early tenants and expectations for these kids. And when others don't agree, they can struggle. But they're unlikely to hold a grudge for too long, as they'd rather make nice and find common ground. In these moments, they learn to tap into their skills of persuasion, using sweetness to get what they want instead.

ADVANCED CONSIDERATIONS

To help clarify the specific nature of a young Libra, it helps to go beyond the sign of their Sun and to look at a little bit more of their birth chart (the planetary snapshot from the minute they were born). As mentioned at the beginning of this book, Venus is a vital planet in determining how a Libra will evolve and show up in the world. It illuminates the driving force and deeper aims of a Libra individual. And what this looks like in Libra's birth chart is one of five potential Venus placements: Venus in Leo, Venus in Virgo, Venus in Libra, Venus in Scorpio, and Venus in Sagittarius. To further enrich one's understanding of a Libra child (also known as a Sun in Libra) we will look at the different nuances each natal Venus sign brings.

VENUS PLACEMENTS

Sun in Libra and Venus in Leo:

Children with Venus in Leo have a distinct need to be self-expressed. While they will still be concerned with fairness and equality, it might be on their own terms. They are learning that they are their own authority and are developing a healthy sense of self to guide their actions. They are likely to have a marked interest in playtime and creative activities, and they crave a sense of the spotlight. As long as their needs are being met, they are inherently warm and generous, but they may also be prone to a dramatic tantrum as they learn how to navigate their disappointments. It is important that they feel special, are given enough attention, and are seen and celebrated for simply being who they are.

Sun in Libra and Venus in Virgo:

Kids with a Virgo Venus long to be seen as helpful and good. They might be more reserved or cautious, feeling a deep need to get things "right." They are very skilled observers and are particularly attuned to language. In their early stages of development, they are likely to greatly appreciate time spent reading and activities focused on learning. They will also have a different need for safety and encouragement. There may be some nervousness or neuroses that need soothing with patience and a calming presence. Teaching these children healthy practices for self-care and acceptance is hugely important. They are often sensitive and very giving to those around them, wanting to be of service. Teaching them hands-on skills and giving them regular and simple responsibilities to take part in will help them feel greater self-worth.

Sun in Libra and Venus in Libra:

With Venus in Libra, there is a pure expression of Libra energy. These kids are highly attuned to others and always seeking connection. They are likely to do a great deal of mirroring, trying on different personas and mimicking the skills of others, to see what fits and how things work. Bonding to parents, siblings, and familiar figures will be wildly meaningful for these children. They will likely have an early appreciation of beauty in the world and are sure to have a sweet tooth. This child longs for a feeling of shared lightness and will struggle with any unfair or uncooperative circumstances. They are likely social at heart and enjoy developing meaningful one-on-one relationships with peers and elders alike.

Sun in Libra and Venus in Scorpio:

Those with Venus in Scorpio show up with more intensity than Libra is typically known for. As kids, these Libras feel things deep to their core. Beyond the joy and beauty of life, they are also looking for meaning early on. They feel a strong pull to the things they enjoy and may go through phases of obsession over their latest delight. They also have the ability to devote themselves to one thing at a time and may not be as free and flighty as some other Libra children. A bit of a stubborn streak sees them drawing boundaries more readily, often in pursuit of truths that are black and white. These children are well served by loyalty and felt attention, and they want to be taken seriously from a very early age.

Sun in Libra and Venus in Sagittarius:

For children born with Venus in Sagittarius, there is a wild vitality to their charming nature. Kids with this placement are likely to be higher energy and have a need to move. They are generally upbeat and outgoing, looking to connect but not to linger. Bike rides, outdoor exploring, storytelling, and the like are all very important here. These Libras are experiential creatures and a little less in their heads than the others. They are looking for fun in their connections and want to learn about life just as much as they want to learn about other people. This lighthearted kiddo wants to keep busy and share in all that the world has to offer us.

LIBRA

as an Adult

Entering adulthood, Libras have spent enough time mirroring and matching their environments. As they continue to individuate, they begin to care less about assimilating and more about discerning. In this phase of their lives, they are looking to reach mastery of right relations, refined taste, and rigorous kindness. In their expanding self-awareness there is a growing capacity for interdependence. They've learned the basics of how to be nice, how to fit in, and how to please, and now they are choosing when, where, and why they do these things.

Shifting their emphasis from connecting to the quality of their connections, Libra adults are learning to wield their sharp and perceptive minds just as much as their charm. Not all associations are worthwhile ones, and connections that might have been superficial but fun in the past no longer sound so appealing. As their experiences accumulate, their values become more clear, and their scales become fine-tuned to these values so that their choices prioritize lasting harmony over short-term ease.

Understanding the weight of time, "easy" and "pleasant" begin to look a little different, too. Libras learn to weigh past, present, and future, maintaining a keen awareness of time in their decision making. Sometimes these layered considerations can delay action, leaving a Libra in a state of stagnation when stakes are high. But ultimately, they are calculating in their best interest, and that may mean that weeks of waiting are better for them than quick decisions they can't take back. Chaos and hurry are to be avoided as often as possible, as any Libra knows that such haste will rob them of their sharp perception and nuanced judgements.

A scale needs time to rebound and reset. If it is unstable or carrying too heavy of a load, it cannot accurately function. And so some Libras may avoid certain decisions or obligations entirely. When something comes up that they deem unwieldy, they can be prone to dodge any ties or responsibilities to it. They know their bandwidth, and the dangers of overloading it, and so they learn how to evade situations or sweetly say no. Whether through delegation, persuasion, or eluding a matter entirely, Libra adults are protective of their energy and intentional about what they take on.

Similarly, they are learning that they need to maintain adequate room for themselves in their connections with others. Once again, focusing on quality, a good companion will advance or reflect their principles and self-worth. As adults, Libras are increasingly learning the importance of their selfhood in how they are able to relate to the world. They are more than just agreeable, and their perspective has equal merit. Having spent a great deal of time studying and evaluating the opinions of others, they are able to put more of a voice to their own thoughts and consider them just as valid.

They also shift from an observer to a witness or an ally. The element of study, of self-reflection and vicarious experience, becomes more neutral as they grow into their own identity. And in that growth they are able to better show up for others. In their own self-rooting, they can see others as they are, with less bias and projection, and hold true space for them. They are able to see the greater web that they are a part of, and tend to it, thread by thread.

This is one of Libra's great gifts—to see each of us and keep us together—to link folks across perceived boundaries and divides. Libras unite disparate parts and create space for the spectrum that lies between two opposing points.

This vision carries with it a real idealism in seeking for honest ease and compromise. There's an air of innocence about them that may have been read early on as simply naivete, as they look for networks that don't yet exist and relations that seem too good to be true. In a world oft unsatisfied by and ill equipped for equity, kindness, and camaraderie, Libra serves as a beacon. They are advocates for advocates and take pride in their belief of human potential. Not only have they learned to look for the best in others, but they have learned that others' light helps to illuminate their own.

However, this truth is hard to carry at all times, and Libras are not immune to doubt and depression. They can become easily overwhelmed and disheartened by harsh realities. In their desire for fairness and grace, the absence of such dynamics can feel like a major burden or hurdle for these adults. And they may struggle to hold the fullness of this, trying to convince themselves of being fine or disassociating from what feels like too much. This is for their own coping needs and self-preservation, but it is also tied to their need to be nice—a need that is asked to evolve in adulthood.

What Libras begin to find is that being nice should never come at the cost of their own integrity. Their conception of kindness deepens over time to recognize that it is not always pleasant or easy. If their goal is to make meaningful relationships and live well, their personal needs have to factor into the equation alongside the needs of others. And once again, the short term must be considered against the long term. Some situations require sacrifices. Some need compromises. Some must be walked away from altogether. And some really are as simple as showing up sincerely. Whatever the situation, Libra needs to call upon their skills of discernment to judge in equal favor of self and other, knowing that the outcome of their actions is just as important as the intention.

This touches on their greater calling as well: justice. Recognizing the importance of their actions and impact, Libra carries the sword of justice throughout their life.

They know fairness from a very early age, but it's generally simplistic. Early on they can be more compromising and less nuanced in determining equality. But in adulthood, their understanding becomes enriched, and they can distinguish when what is deemed fair is not also just. Justice speaks when the scales are not enough. It cuts through appearances and weighs the intangible, the unspeakable. It is the culmination of reason and wisdom. It is the gift of a Libra in alignment with their power.

And feeding this power is their eternal softness. Their sensitivity to beauty, pleasure, kindness. Tools that the world might see as luxuries, the Libra knows are birthrights. They seek out joy and indulgence in the everyday. They treasure their rest, belongings, style, and connections. They appreciate the sweetness of their bonds and the honey of time spent with others. Well-appointed rooms become sanctuaries. A good book can become simple medicine. Pleasure is pursued ardently because they know it is paramount. They know that ease is vital, achievable, and most likely to bring one into bloom.

Libra adults are the peacekeepers. They are persuasively passive and gently engaging. As eager accomplices, they are folks looking to lighten the load for all of us. They are giving and receiving, pausing and passing, negotiating at every turn so as to keep us comfortably afloat. Keepers of kind words, they encourage us to trust in grace and trust in each other. Libra reminds us that we are inextricably connected and that our bonds to each other are often our greatest teachers.

ADVANCED CONSIDERATIONS

Having addressed the general temperament for Libra adults, it's time to get specific. Each Libra Sun has their own unique character, and Venus plays a big role in shaping that. Read on for each of the different blends and Libra styles.

VENUS PLACEMENTS

Sun in Libra and Venus in Leo:

As adults, Libras with Venus in Leo are warm and gregarious creatures. They have a dramatic flair and unique charm.

Their values are founded upon a strong sense of self, and they know that they have something special to offer others. Folks are drawn to their radiant energy and uplifted by their partnership. These Libras must be ever mindful of the balance between their own persistent desires and the wants and needs of those around them. While they are generally ones to share the wealth, sometimes their egos and grandiose nature can get the best of them, and they put their persuasive skills to work for their own ends rather than others' interests. A healthy ego keeps them in check about when to compromise and when to put on their crown instead.

Sun in Libra and Venus in Virgo:

Adults with Venus in Virgo are greatly service oriented. They live very much in their heads, led by a distinctly practical nature and sense of reason. There may be a tendency toward anxiousness here, but there is also a highly refined capacity for discernment. These Libras make exacting critics, for better and for worse, often seeing themselves as their greatest work in progress. There is a constant striving and reaching for perfection made real here. And with their meticulous eye, these folks are able to cultivate and refine incredible systems in their lives and our world. They feel most at ease when they are serving a clear purpose or tangibly doing good. Sometimes this leads them to give to exhaustion, but being the efficient people they are, they know when and how to self-care themselves back to vibrant health.

Sun in Libra and Venus in Libra:

For Libra adults with Venus in their own sign, there is a natural grace and sensitivity to aesthetics. They are well-mannered and charming folks who have a strong sense of ethics. Their desire for balance sees them prioritizing leisure and simplicity, embodying an air of minimalism. But they also know how to show up meaningfully for others, with little tolerance for injustice in the world. They're quite equipped to "kill 'em with kindness," as they know that their greatest gift is softness. By modeling a gentle nature and devotion to harmony and ease, this Libra reflects to the world how smooth things could be. These folks are also likely to hold a very wide perspective of the world and to be quite astute. Their minds are sensitive and sharp, looking for fairness wherever possible. Silver-tongued, they are often able to tip the scales in favor of their choosing.

Sun in Libra and Venus in Scorpio:

The Libra with a Scorpio Venus grows up to be quite a force. They are unable to be as complacent as some of their other Libra brethren can be. Rather than simple ease, they are also inclined to prioritize depth. They look for bonds that will be lasting and total, commitments that are more than just pretty. This is the Libra with fierce loyalty and cunning charm. They are nice to a point, but they won't tolerate too many superficialities. There is a sense of longing in this Libra, a hunger that propels them and never quite goes away. And there is also a desire to be reborn and transformed through their relationship to the world and to others. This can show up through their appearance, taking on a new look with each phase they find themselves in. They are also a Libra who can use and witness pain to inspire new and more authentic pleasures.

Sun in Libra and Venus in Sagittarius:

As adults, Libras with Venus in Sagittarius pack an exuberant punch. They have both a liveliness and a depth that goes beyond Libra's general sociability. There's an urge for them to know and see more about their fellow man, looking for ties and similarities that cross boundaries and hold us all together. They are often idealists and driven by philosophy and myth. These Libras are able to use stories and experiences to bring people closer. Employing joy, vibrancy, and an inspired charm, they are able to cultivate many allies and a shared sense of hope and adventure. For this Libra, there may be more peace in movement than in being still. They are pulled by promise and potential and reach for that in their partnerships. And with their confidence and goofy grin, they're often able to bring out the brightest in folks.

LIBRA

as a Parent

Being the innate partners they are, Libras bring a tender set of skills to the role of parenting. The job is inherently relational and dynamic, and thus Libra, in many ways, has an edge. Be it with co-parent, child, sibling, teachers—whoever—parenting is inundated with relationships and shared agreements. And in these aspects, a Libra parent can really shine.

Libras work hard to cultivate and maintain meaningful relationships, and this is even more true for those who choose to parent, especially for their children. They hold a unique ability to partner with and uplift their kids from a very early age. With babies, Libras exercise their mastery of mirroring and are sharply attuned to the needs and development of their children. Their ability to identify with the experience of others is wildly useful and keeps them rather sympathetic to their kin.

They are also able to witness and listen for what is needed. Their kids benefit from considerate attention and a genuine curiosity from their parents. Libras are wired to thoroughly engage with the folks around them and look to build connections. Consequently, they can become pretty linked to their children, always wanting to share in each other's worlds.

This parent also wants to encourage and experience the true nature of their kiddos. These are parents who can generally allow their children to feel comfortable just as they are. With great care given to developing a bond, they can be very accommodating. But that is also where they need to be careful. Libra parents must make sure that they allow enough space for proper individuation. And they also need to remember that they are parent more than friend. While Libras love to be loved, they will be faced with tough calls and asked to lay down the law for their kids, whether folks like it or not. They must be diligent in prioritizing their child's well-being over any sneaking desire to be lenient or "chill."

And on the flip side, they should be wary of any desire to shape or groom their child in their own image. Since they want the best for their kids, and their conception of this is ease and grace, they may try to soften or gloss over any perceived rough spots. A rebellious or offbeat nature might worry the Libra parent, who just wishes their child were universally liked. If these parents find themselves trying to subtly maneuver or shape their kids, they must examine their motives and allow for the quirks and awkward moments to exist.

This is not to say, however, that they can't still make their family's lives more appealing in other ways. Their eye for style is likely to be evident throughout their home and lifestyle. From well-appointed bedrooms to tasteful toys and apparel, Libras keep their kin looking sharp. They are often parents who love to shop and dress their children in fine things. It is important to them to be surrounded by style whenever possible, and they share these gifts with their family and kids.

They also know the value of quality rest and care. So beyond the looks, they work hard to make sure their family feels luxurious, too. These parents may be strict on bedtime, or just lax on when their littles wake up, as good sleep is paramount in their world. It is important to them that their kids are well rested and get adequate time to relax. These parents are stress averse, and they'll step in when they see their kids' energy slip from accommodating to simply drained. In moments of high worry or strain, these Libras are able to swoop in with a well-timed treat or break from excessive demands. They do all that they can to keep a manageable and pleasant pace.

Schedules stay well maintained, too, with these parents. Their exquisite sense of balance helps them to navigate the many demands of the day, and they keep their kids comfortably busy. Depending on the Libra, it may look like a daily checklist that's flexible but clear, or it could function best as a precise schedule, interwoven with both rest and obligations. Whatever their personal style, all Libra parents are able to call upon their acute understanding of time to help them take on their days. It makes them great prioritizers and excellent planners, unlikely to break a sweat.

Mealtime is another important marker for these parents, and for some, may be the star of the day. Libras care most about connection, and there are few better places to get caught up and take it easy than around a shared meal. The food itself is likely to be light, fresh, and satisfying, as Libra parents like to instill in their families the virtues of a well-balanced diet. And while they may not always be the ones cooking it, as some can't be bothered, they'll certainly be the ones providing and prioritizing it. Social and inviting, meals are a place for their family to take a breath and enjoy all that is at and around the table.

They also take advantage of shared time to further model to their children graciousness and good behavior. Libras take it upon themselves to demonstrate kindness and ease in most all that they do, and parenting amplifies this behavior. Seeing that they are natural observers themselves, they know intimately how much we are influenced by the people around us. And they use this as a rule of thumb with their kids. They strive to model not only considerate behavior, but also attentive self-care. Libra parents need to be sure to give as much to themselves as they do to others, because when they don't, their kids will struggle to learn this lesson, too.

Another facet of the Libra parent is that they are excellent negotiators. Whether through allowances or reward, compromise or contract, these Libras aren't afraid to use their charm to outsmart their kids. Or their partners. Co-parents are expected to pull their fair share in the rearing of children, and one way that Libras maintain this is through regular and objective agreements. Tasks, chores, and responsibilities are to be distributed evenly throughout their house, and when the balance falters these Libras hold court. They are stern but reasonable, offering equal reward for an honest effort.

Chaotic periods can overload these parents, though, and try as they might, it can't always be prevented. This is where their network becomes very important to their family. When these parents become overworked or over-whelmed, they need windows of rest to recalibrate and keep their cool. A Libra without the ability to recharge often falls flat and can feel paralyzed by their immediate environment. They need partners who can step in when they're fading, as well as friends and community to help take the lead, too. It's important they learn to share their responsibilities and are able to build a team of folks to help their family succeed. From nannies, to neighbors, to elders, to a coach, these parents work their web of connections to keep their days as breezy as they can. Libras come to find that parenting well shared is parenting well done.

ADVANCED CONSIDERATIONS

Once again, every Libra has their own subtleties, and this is where we get a little more specific. Having spoken thoroughly about the Libra Sun on its own, it's now time to look into the different styles based on their Venus placement.

VENUS PLACEMENTS

Sun in Libra and Venus in Leo:

With Venus in Leo, these Libra parents put their big hearts on display and are proud and cheerful. They're likely to make great playmates and keep things fun. But they must remember to balance their own identity with their role as parent and be clear on how they prioritize their children. If they are able to maintain their own unique style and sense of self, they are not only happier but also able to be incredible role models for self-care. It is key that they find healthy ways to feel special outside of their parenting. In knowing this about themselves and cultivating such opportunities, they're easily able to help their kids feel just as grand and important. They are great cheerleaders and rather affectionate, voicing their love and admiration often. And in their relationships, when co-parenting, they are learning a similar balance of celebrating the skills that each person brings to the table. As long as they are keeping any bouts of inflated ego or self-importance in check, their confidence and kindness makes them affable and adoring parents.

Sun in Libra and Venus in Virgo:

Libra parents with Venus in Virgo are tender caretakers and teachers. They parent from a place of altruism, and work hard to create the best environment and opportunities for their kin. This parent gives tremendously and needs to be mindful of any tendency to martyr. It is important that they are able to keep some sense of routine, and they are wise to impart this skill on their children. This is also a parent who is good with the details. They know how to maintain a schedule and keep up with a bevy of tasks. The Virgo Venus is skilled at implementing strategies and spotting inefficiencies. It can make them prone to becoming a little too critical at times or hung up on things being done a certain way, but it also means that they respond well to feedback and want very much to be seen as exceptional parents.

Whether it's with partners or through avid reading of parenting books, this Libra most succeeds when maintaining clear dialogue around the shifting needs and strategies of their household.

Sun in Libra and Venus in Libra:

As Sun and Venus in Libra parents, the sweet spot is in keeping things sweet. These parents bring the fullness of the Libra archetype into their parenting and work to create balanced bonds with their kids. They are curious and careful with their children, noting the many ways they are similar and different, and savoring each note. These parents are very open and hope to learn just as much from their kids as they teach. They love the exchange, working to foster trust and softness in their relating. This goes for any co-parents as well. Parenting is viewed as a team effort, so they not only encourage their partners to have their own clear role, but they expect it. They value their children having access to varied perspectives and keep a calm and open-minded household. Tolerance and acceptance are prioritized, along with comfort and peace. And still the aesthete, they enjoy surrounding their kids with art and beauty, looking to enliven their little ones' sense of style at an early age.

Sun in Libra and Venus in Scorpio:

With Venus in Scorpio, the Libra parent shows up with a deep sense of devotion to their role. These parents are passionate and love their littles with a great intensity. They can be more protective than other Libras, and due to their depths, they're not always so free and easy. There is an edge to their softness, as they want more than just nice for themselves and their family. This is a parent that has a need for influence and will teach their children about power dynamics, whether through words or actions. They are also more guarded and likely to be private in certain respects around their household. They strive to have an impactful bond with their children and are more in tune with the subtleties of their nature. Highly intuitive, this parent is able to pick up on emotions and hold tender space for their kids. It is important, however, that this skill does not become invasive and that these parents grant their children the same degree of privacy that they demand for themselves.

Sun in Libra and Venus in Sagittarius:

Libra parents with Venus in Sagittarius bring a bright enthusiasm and zeal to the table. These parents are eager to play and make meaning with their children, sharing stories and teaching them about the wider world. They want their kids to have reach and meaningful understanding of other cultures and lifestyles. This is also the parent that takes trips and cultivates learning experiences. They are hands-on and invite their children to engage with life in a similar fervor. It is important that these parents watch for any dogmatic tendencies, however, and that they stay open to their kids' unique truths and perspectives. Additionally, these parents need to be mindful of their buoyancy and pace, as their children may be more emotional or reserved and in need of more sensitivity and patience. The gift these parents bring is that of inspiration and amusement. As for the more tedious needs and responsibilities, they may rely on a steadier co-parent to help see those boxes get checked.

LIBRA

in Love

ove. A topic unique to every sign, but wildly dear to the Libra Sun. It is the driving force for many, as it is the gift of Venus. Goddess of Love, the planet of connection—Venus is always in love, and so, too, are Venus's kin. For Libra, it is very much about being in love with the idea of love. Being in pursuit of love's essence and air. Getting lost in the motions of it and the pleasures they can bring.

It is also so much bigger than romantic love. Libras know this well. For the sign of the scales, all love is vital, and equal, and important. Friendships, family, self, partners— all relationships are to be held on sacred grounds, and all relationships have the potential to teem with love.

While not always so serious or dreamy in practice, these idealized notions are still at the core of any Libra. They never want to be in short supply of sweetness, and so they remain open to connection at every turn. Libras model grace and acceptance to others not only as a tool but as an offering. And it is for themselves just as much as anyone else.

In love, Libra is enlivened and soothed. It lights them up and helps them feel whole. The feeling also brings out their charm in full force. Their style is flirty, playful, alluring, and bright. Eager to connect, but just as happy to tease and taunt, they are quite social and amusing with their affection. Their airy nature enjoys lightheartedness, potential, and fantasy. They can be coy and subtle, looking to captivate and enchant rather than making any big moves. Libras in love long to be sought after and pursued, luring folks in like honey.

And however beguiling, it is also sincere. A Libra can truly be in love with anyone or anything. Maybe not for long, or with much depth, but as a concept, a state of mind, Libras drift into love often. And from this place, they are drawn to different types of love to meet their different needs from love. It is unlikely that a Libra would be satisfied by only one meaningful relationship in their life, however nice it may sound to some. They need diversity of attention and affection; they need the fresh and new. They need best friends as much as they need lovers or business partners or kids. Balance in love given and received is vital, and it comes from many sources.

This element of platonic love is woven throughout all of Libra's relationships. Again, love is very much an idea, an ideal, for this sign. And it is Libra's work to make the ideal as real as it can be. Kind natured, amiable, and attentive, they reach others in such a tender and simple way. They make themselves approachable and easy to know, and they find common ground wherever possible. It is their gift to find the threads that link us, no matter how small or faint. But that is also where they must be careful.

In bringing such ease into the lives of those they love, they sometimes lose sight of who they are in their own right. Libras can get lost in love, thinking that it exists outside of themselves or only when they behave some kind of way. They can so easily give away or subdue certain parts of themselves to make others more comfortable. In certain moments, this ability has its advantages, but ultimately, it keeps them from the love they need and deserve. Libras must learn to love themselves and to remember that love is shared. If they are not receiving as much as they give, they need to find another way to balance the scales.

It can be helpful for them to remember and call upon

their element of air. Thanks to this element, Libras have the potential to merge love with reason, a capacity that keeps them impartial. And in the early stages of love, it is important that they keep their head. Their ability to be rational informs their ability to be kind, and when they lose sight of what's real, they can be caught making allowances that aren't fair to themselves. They are wise to lean on and love up their friends just as much as any new crush, as they might need other folks to help maintain their common sense when feelings get involved.

In general, Libra is not a sign that feels feelings so much as one that thinks about them. They can spin out and lose focus in the day to day, as too many emotions can start to cloud their thoughts. And this clouding doesn't help with their propensity for indecision. It can be hard for them to make major commitments, or at least to make the right commitments for themselves. Where love's concerned, some Libras struggle to remember that immediate gratification often comes at the cost of something more enduring, and vice versa. This dilemma brings up the issue of quality versus quantity for them, too.

Libras can get swept up in others' advances and say yes to every offer. They love the newness of puppy love and infatuation, and they feel good being so wanted. This can mean that some Libras look for all the relationships and flings that they can find. However, what they want to be able to receive and to give then comes into question. Quantity is great if it makes a Libra feel vibrant and loved. But when it's not great is when a Libra gets burnt out or is unable to connect to the degree they want. Libras need to practice discernment in their love lives in order to stay balanced and aligned with their personal values.

And despite certain opinions, Libras can date any other zodiac sign they want. In fact, all of the signs can date anyone they want, and Libra should know this best. There are many types of relationships that can be had and many types of people under every Sun sign. Libras should let go of any idea that they should be with one over another. It's best they stay open to the reality of how others show up and make them feel in practice rather than on paper. Folks of any sign that celebrate, respect, and adore their Libra make a good match for the scales.

ADVANCED CONSIDERATIONS

Looking into Libras in love, it is even more important to consider their Venus sign. As we are learning to note how each Libra Sun is altered by their Venus placement, it is twofold in regards to love. Seeing that Venus is the ruler of the sign Libra and the planet of love itself, its placement is so important to understanding this point. Below we examine how Venus brings a distinct style of connection for Libras in love.

VENUS PLACEMENTS

Sun in Libra and Venus in Leo:

Venus in Leo is looking for a grand love. Big gestures, bright sparks, and total devotion. Love that is warm and inspired. They have excellent taste and like to share the wealth. Giving and receiving gifts is often a facet of their love language. They are also generous with their time for the ones they love. Their loyalty is lasting and bold, and they never forget a kind favor or brightened day. Compliments don't hurt either, as they love to feel celebrated and special. Their beloveds are expected to be demonstrative, and in return they get to share in the hearty glow of this Libra's affection.

They can be rather sovereign, too, and often need to feel that they are seated on the throne of their lover's heart. Whether in love with one, with none, or with many, these Libras need to know that they are the most important person to any serious admirer.

Sun in Libra and Venus in Virgo:

For Venus in Virgo, love is demonstrated through acts of service. Love is an action. A favor granted, a chore completed, an errand run. It is patient and pragmatic, grounded in true care. These Libras pay avid attention to their loved ones' needs, and they work hard to make sure they are met. They note nuances and preferences and get all the details just right, often an encyclopedia for the likes and dislikes of their beloveds. And in return, their heart sings upon acknowledgement of their diligence and service. Hearty thank-yous, naming, and witnessing how well they keep things together is often more than enough for their humble hearts. Affirming words can make them swoon. That and also tangible time, which can be spent talking or problem solving together, working on a shared project, or making a meal together. These Libras appreciate a simple moment shared. They can be nervous in love and hard to settle down, but underneath their busyness, their hearts yearn to feel valued and adored for their modesty.

Sun in Libra and Venus in Libra:

With Venus in Libra, there is a desire for that first spark, for the newness that connection brings. These are the coy flirts and polished lovers, emanating a cool grace in their every move. This Libra is looking for a fluid and easy exchange in their relationships. They are very accommodating and able to meet folks in the middle in the name of love. And they're a sucker for sweet talk. A good conversation, a playful bout of banter, a letter from their admirer—they wanna hear the love. Through charming appearances, these Libras look to entice others with their lively allure and have an earnest but measured approach. Often quick to bond, they are not necessarily quick to commit or get serious. While some enjoy a steady fling, plenty of these Libras like to date around just as much, basking in the glow of infatuation and new romance. And beyond the romance, these Libras are just as likely to be in love with their friends and community. With Venus in Libra, every relationship is an opportunity to share in loving affection and pleasant harmony.

Sun in Libra and Venus in Scorpio:

For the Libra with Venus in Scorpio, love is eternal, powerful, moving. These Libras carry profound feelings and can get hooked on others. They want to be transformed by love, remade again and again in its image. They are also very loyal, with a fierce devotion to those they love. Ease can feel a little difficult, or rather disinteresting for these Libras, as they tend to equate love with intensity. Ardent and passionate, they are often boiling underneath their cool exteriors. They may vacillate between playing hard to get and then inundating their loves with affection, sometimes struggling with knowing or trusting what they want. But when they do know, they allow their loves to become their world. These are the Libras who yearn for intimacy over flighty flirts and want love to claim them and reveal hidden worlds. Their brand of charm is synonymous with seduction and is infused with magnetism, charisma, and allure.

Sun in Libra and Venus in Sagittarius:

Libras with Venus in Sagittarius prefer a grand and rowdy kind of love. Using their charm to sweep folks off their feet, these Libras steal hearts wherever they roam. They enjoy the pursuit and are after experiences more than maintenance, looking most for impulsive and wild fun. They find love in movement and adventure and share it best with the folks who can help them find such states. Unafraid to take a risk, these Libras are more likely to speak out and share their hearts, captivating others with their visions. They are lighthearted and inspirational, goofy and free. These Libras view love as a journey and look for those most willing to take the trip. It is important to them that love reflects their ideals and that their connections have a sense of purpose. They can be high-minded and philosophical, and they need bonds that are on the same page, looking to make meaning that is well beyond the here and now.

RISING SIGNS

In addition to one's Venus placement, there are a number of factors that make each Libra unique. Another layer to the birth chart, a placement we all have, is the ascendant or rising sign. Based on when and where a Libra was born, their ascendant reflects the sign that was rising on the horizon, and it is tied to where the Sun sat in the sky at the moment of their birth. This component of a birth chart is greatly important and informative, but for now, we will just be looking at how it influences a Libra in love. This is another layer that sits on top of the nuance that one's Venus placement provides.

Aries Rising and Sun in Libra:

With Aries rising, these Libras know how to go after what they want, and they enjoy a bit of chase and drama in love. They can also be quick to catch feelings and expect a relationship to help them stay balanced. They're drawn to folks who are well mannered and alluring, with social charm in spades.

Taurus Rising and Sun in Libra:

For the Taurus rising Libra, their love needs a little more intensity, with partners that aren't afraid to commit. They look for loves that are meaty and complex, allowing them to explore their hidden impulses. A fan of the slow burn, they're also willing to let love throw them a little off-balance if it means they get to share in another's depths.

Gemini Rising and Sun in Libra:

As a Gemini rising Libra, the emphasis is entirely on flirty fun and adventure. They are drawn to bold types, smooth talkers, and any cutie with enough charm. These Libras live for inspired romance and want to be swept off their feet. They're likely to date freely, always up for a good time.

Cancer Rising and Sun in Libra:

With Cancer rising, Libras long for a little extra tenderness and want a love that is committed and stable. These Libras are more reserved and take relationships seriously, looking for mature partners that they can grow roots with. Love for this Libra looks like showing up on time, following through on promises, and having immense integrity.

Leo Rising and Sun in Libra:

Leo rising Libras have a bright yet cool air in love. They want to be noticed for their charm, but they don't mind when somebody plays a little hard to get. They're drawn to confident types that have their own distinct style and can offer something unique. In relationships, they like somebody that's not intimidated by their vibrant glow.

Virgo Rising and Sun in Libra:

With Virgo rising, Libras long to be enchanted and transported by love. They can come off as a little reserved or straightlaced, but they're just waiting for the right lovers to unlock their dreamier side. These Libras are drawn to folks with deep compassion and big hearts, and they are impressed by partners that can bring their fantasies to life.

Libra Rising and Sun in Libra:

For the double Libra (with Sun and rising) they like their loves with a little heat. As they are effortlessly considerate and always keeping things together, they're easily pulled in by the bold and brash. They like partners that take charge and bring out their fire. These Libras often look to their relationships to remind them of their own independence and unique spark.

Scorpio Rising and Sun in Libra:

With Scorpio rising, a Libra is looking for love to keep them grounded. They're drawn to slow and steady types that bring out their indulgent side and shower them in pleasure. These Libras are looking for love to bring release, to get them out of their heads, and root them more in their own bodies and hearts.

Sagittarius Rising and Sun in Libra:

Sagittarius rising Libras are likely to root their loves in friendship first. They like partners that feel light and easy and prioritize fun. This is a Libra that wants a dynamic, open, multifaceted love. They can bore easily, so they've got to be kept on their toes and well entertained. Confident, quirky, and delightfully quick-witted is the type to win over their hearts.

Capricorn Rising and Sun in Libra:

For the Libra with Capricorn rising, love is meant to be lasting, tender, and true. Their relationships need a certain degree of grace and sensitivity and should feel secure, with sturdy roots. These Libras need lovers they can confide in and rest easy with. They might also seek connections that look good on paper, but if they don't feel good, too, they're not likely to last long.

Aquarius Rising and Sun in Libra:

With Aquarius rising, these Libras are looking for lovers that indulge and inspire their ideals. They're rather friendly and open-minded and are in search of the connections that fill their hearts and make them feel special. Relationships bring out their dramatic side and see them enjoying bold declarations and sharing big gestures. In love they prioritize play, humor, and self-expression.

Pisces Rising and Sun in Libra:

Libras with Pisces rising like a love that keeps things together. These Libras have a dreamy depth to them and look for partners that are attentive and kind. They are drawn to the smart, sensitive, and charitable. Love for these Libras is selfless, patient, considerate, kind; they long to feel safe and well cared for.

LIBRA

at Work

For the sign of Libra, work needs to be sweeter than it is for most. In what is often a place of drudgery and stress, with either busyness or boredom dominating, Libra Suns look to shine a soothing light. These are the folks that keep people calm and connected, that put difficulties into perspective, and that find small ways to infuse their work with pleasure.

They note birthdays and plan coffee breaks. They listen and hold space. They make the mundane feel easy rather than stifling. These are the bright and attentive employees who aim to please and keep the team on even keel. And thanks to their geniality, they find many opportunities and excel in a number of roles.

Libras are natural negotiators for one. They know what's fair, and they know what others want. They can appeal to a wide range of people, and they gain favor with their cordial manner, softening folks into compromise. This also serves them well in a court and other facets of the legal system. Libras are well attuned to the law and skilled at enforcing it, as long as they deem it just. And when they find fault in the law, or in others, they advocate and work for change. They utilize their sharp minds to work to dismantle systems that they see failing.

Often seen in roles that connect them to people in need, their work tends to be quite relational, and they are most fulfilled by being in connection with others. So even if it's not in service or advocacy work, it may be that they deal with clients or have a business partner, or maybe they work as an assistant. It can also be that they relate to ideas. Libras with artistic leanings make excellent curators or designers. And others make for highly skilled writers. Whatever the role, the emphasis is on mental engagement, meaningful connections, and the ability to find joy in what they do.

Libras also have a very real need for balance in their work lives. What is an aspiration for some is more often a requirement for a Libra, at least if they want to sustain their efforts and commitment. Libras need to be careful not to overexert themselves. They have their own pace and will need to find work that is suited to it. They also need breaks spread throughout the day and the right mix of tasks. All day spent on one thing is likely to get old quick for a Libra. It's easier for them to divide their time, alternating between the more enjoyable tasks and the strenuous or menial.

They may also need an equal blend of time spent working with others and working alone. While they may tend to lean into more social engagement than less, too much, especially at work, can zap their energy or fog up their own sensibilities. They need enough windows throughout their day to return to themselves and clear their minds. Their ability to collaborate and merge into a project or partner can be very powerful, but it is just as liable to see them lose touch with their own needs and to burn out.

A daily errand that often keeps them in balance is meals. Having good coffee or tea, stepping out to a favorite cafe, grabbing a snack—the little indulgences these moments provide help a Libra feel at ease. And they also allow for rebalancing. For the Libra that works alone, a simple outing allows for meeting a friend or flirting with a barista to get their social fix. And for those who need a break, it's an opportunity to slow down, find solitude, and recharge. Plus, the right treat can upgrade any moment.

And for the Libras less interested in indulgence via tangible treats, there's always the internet. Libras are pros at online shopping their way through a slow day or boring meeting. Scrolling through the news and social media helps to distract them from any unpleasant realities on the job and keeps their minds busy. As do chats and messages with coworkers or friends. For the Libra that doesn't like what they do, they find creative ways to look busy while keeping up to date on what they deem to be more interesting matters.

Similarly, Libras are pretty good at keeping up to date on office matters, too. Details like birthdays, anniversaries, and holiday planning are often opportunities for a Libra to do something nice at work. They're great at leaving notes or sending cards, and they're even better at planning an office party. Combining their refined style, love of leisure, abundant social graces, and a need to make our days more agreeable, they make work gatherings feel good. These folks are the champions of a mixer and are almost always thrilled to blend work and play. But if lines get crossed or work doesn't get finished, Libras can also flex their loyalty to all that is fair.

While they can be known to bend a rule or two in their

own favor, generally their ethics are impartial and rules are rules. Libras will keep their clients and coworkers accountable and expect them to be just as honorable as they are. They also expect equal contributions. Few things irk them more than a peer that tries to ride on the coattails of another's hard work. Libras expect their associates to do their part and share in the labor.

When justice needs to be served, Libras are stern but kind. They know how to keep their cool with fussy clients and arrogant collaborators. And as much as they can, they seek to encourage and motivate. They rarely lead with a firm boundary and much prefer when they can incite folks to change through gentle words and thoughtful attention. But when their graciousness is not enough, they are able to cut through other's boorish behavior and lay out clear expectations in a cool and assured manner.

ADVANCED CONSIDERATIONS

It's time to dive a little deeper and look at how Venus placements influence the energy of Libras at work. While the general Libra descriptions provide a great overview, this layer adds a more accurate and individual tone. Look below to see how the different Venus signs affect Libras in their trades.

VENUS PLACEMENTS

Sun in Libra and Venus in Leo:

For the Libra with Venus in Leo, work is yet another place that they get to offer their shine. These Libras do well in charge and can lead by example, with a gentle confidence that others trust. They are likely to be rather creative, and many make great performers. Even if they're a little reserved, they have a need to be seen as gifted in the work that they do, and they respond well to praise for their efforts and offerings. A little prestige doesn't hurt either, so if they're not in a literal spotlight, it might be a title that they're after or an award of recognition. These Libras also make great coworkers, keeping the energy open and fun, with a slight taste for office gossip. Their easy charm brings out folk's gregariousness and can attract loyal clients. And while they're very generous in their work, they are not ones to go underpaid or overlooked. These Libras have no problem naming their needs and seeing that they are met.

Sun in Libra and Venus in Virgo:

Libras with Venus in Virgo are skilled researchers and social servants. They are very adept at law and legislation and have a penchant for tedious arts. Working with their hands can help offset their busy and restless minds, and it is likely to keep them grounded on the job. They may also have a penchant for working with nature, perhaps as gardeners or herbalists. These folks are able to retain an exhaustive amount of information about the topics that most interest them, and their eye for details helps them apply their insights in apt and meaningful ways. They are likely to be specialists in their field of work. Libras tend to keep the ship afloat when no one's looking. They keep tidy, run errands, send cards, fix the paper jam, and probably work longer hours than they're asked to.

Sun in Libra and Venus in Libra:

As a Libra with Venus in the same sign, there is a natural propensity for working with and for others. Be it advocacy work, social work, client management, or counseling, these folks need engagement with others in their jobs. They care about people deeply and are dedicated to cultivating harmony and equality for all. Especially in one-to-one settings. These Libras care about the connection and are most effective when they can work directly with another person. They are also quite skilled in law, with an acute sense of right and wrong, and the persuasive skills to gently win the nastiest of arguments. Serving as consultants or coordinators are intuitive roles for their skillset as well. They are able to keep folks connected and calm. And of course, any job imbued with beauty and keen on aesthetics suits them as well. They bring style to all that they do.

Sun in Libra and Venus in Scorpio:

With Venus in Scorpio, Libras bring a real tenacity to their work. They are drawn to people and look to make a lasting impact more than superficial. They are often advocates for underdogs, outcasts, survivors, and the overlooked. They want their work to reach those who need it most, and they'll work tirelessly to do so. These Libras are highly motivated, looking for a calling more than just a job. They're the ones to fixate on a passion project or fiercely climb the ladder of success. It is important for them to feel that they have influence in their work and in the world. They need to feel that they are impactful. And they also provide a depth of care that not all Libras can. There is an innate awareness to others' wounding and a desire to help folks transform and overcome adversity. As a soft yet brutal force, they channel their intensity with charm and ease.

Sun in Libra and Venus in Sagittarius:

Libras with Venus in Sagittarius bring with them a vivaciousness to work. These Libras are a little freer and wilder and are drawn to a higher calling. They want to feel that their work is meaningful and aligned with their vision of truth. Looking to inspire and be inspired, they are less bound by commitment and more bound by faith. They are also the storytellers and seekers, and may find success in entertainment, international relations, philosophy, and travel. Jobs that keep them on the road and meeting new people are well suited to their nature. They want some excitement and enjoy having a platform to speak about their beliefs. They're also likely to be improvisational and quite spirited in their work. Keeping the office lighthearted and energized is their speciality.

6

LIBRA

in School

While school can be a divisive place for some, Libras are likely to find a number of ways to enjoy it. It's a pivotal place for making connections and sharing ideas, both in youth and adulthood, and those experiences are lifelong Libra needs. As social, chatty people, this setting is ideal and provides a good container for this sign to grow within.

Not all Libras will be particularly studious, however. Depending on one's individual values, there can be a preference for the social aspects over the scholarly, while others will thrive in the intellectual setting or work hard to please parents, teachers, and collaborators. Each scale is calibrated differently, and educational settings can help illuminate a Libra's specific bent. A shared experience amongst all Libras, however, can be a sense of weariness or anxiety from the school setting. As the environment demands a lot from Libra's attention, the scales are put on high alert, with little time to rest in the face of overstimulation. A Libra in any social setting for too long, especially an intellectual and institutional one, can easily lose sight of themselves and burn out in their endless adjusting to the dynamic scene.

Without a clear sense of personal order, there are too many judgements to be made. Their minds can be overwrought with questions well before a lecture begins. Should they sit with their friends? Get caught up on gossip? Do they need a good grade, or can they coast this one out? Do they even care about this topic? And if they don't, should they? Especially in their younger days, Libras can get easily distracted in the classroom when they haven't figured out what's important to them. For this reason, they frequently learn best through other people.

From tutors to teachers to a well-written biography, Libra is most likely to be pulled in by people and information that is made directly relatable. They do well with a study buddy and other folks to keep them both interested and accountable. Libras also enjoy having other people to talk to and explore ideas with. They like a good exchange and use the back-and-forth to help them feel out ideas and hear things from other perspectives. For many, it also stirs their interest in debate. Libras are quite skilled at understanding how and why arguments are won and can see things from all sides.

Other skills and subjects that call to Libras are art, social studies, literature, and the humanities. They excel in the subjects that allow them to appreciate subtlety, take in great beauty, and note associations. They enjoy topics built on symmetries and human stories. Any information that helps them to better understand and feel akin to their fellow humans is of great value to Libra. And beyond the classroom, school life itself is a place where these connections can be explored.

Regardless of their scene, a school is an important place for Libras to foster and find relationships. This can happen with just one great teacher for some, and for others, they're the belle of the ball, with plenty of social attention. For the lone Libra in school, they will sniff out relationships to help them get through the day. They find ties to clubs or teams, pick up a tutor, get to know their counselor, or just hang exclusively with their BFF. Whatever their style, Libras need at least one relationship they can count on to help get through the school day. And more likely than not, they are able to find a number of folks to keep them connected.

Another matter for Libras to sort out at school is figuring out what they want to do. Libras can take a while to get clarity on what sort of studies or education most inspires them. They like to weigh all the options before committing to just one path. Some Libras may never look to specialize, and some may find themselves merging two different paths, finding ways to link discordant topics in order to best suit their skills and interests. Others may just be interested in what's easy, as their school experience is focused on making friends and just managing to gently get through it all.

To make school easier, Libras can learn to lean into their air sign gifts. Whether it's writing, speaking, or just connecting the dots, every Libra has some sort of mental prowess. Many Libras excel in expressing their thoughts via pen and paper. Writing allows Libras to plan out and organize their ideas, putting to work their skills of persuasion with their inherent sense of symmetry. It's also helpful for them to write down notes and to use this skill as a study tool.

Another side of their airy nature, however, is distractibility. Libras need to make sure they give themselves enough space to try out new ideas and pursue different strategies. Within their work, they need to allow themselves the freedom to make mistakes and explore. Maintaining curiosity is important if they want to stay engaged. And within their school experiences, they need opportunities to bounce ideas around and hear other insights. Sometimes taking a break or trying a new skill can spark fresh connections when they're feeling stifled or stuck.

In fact, fresh starts and sudden changeups help activate their cardinal nature and open them up to inspiration. Tapping into this energy can help them succeed, but they should be mindful of launching too many new projects that they can't see through. Libras are great at starting things, but they can struggle with completing them. When the urge to abandon a responsibility strikes, it could be a good idea for the Libra to set in place some rewards for completing their more bothersome tasks.

ADVANCED CONSIDERATIONS

When it comes to school, all Libras have a shared style, but factoring in their Venus sign illuminates a range of specialities. By looking at their Venus placement, we can see where the Libra student is more likely to be pulled in and find success. Let's examine the different natures of each Libra scholar as influenced by their Venus.

VENUS PLACEMENTS

Sun in Libra and Venus in Leo:

For the Libra with Venus in Leo, creative outlets are key. These folks have an expressive nature and learn best when they are able to see content as personally relevant or interesting. They are often drawn in and captivated by the big personalities in history, connecting with bold leaders and courageous hearts. And they work best with mentors and teachers that carry a strong sense of self and that will name and encourage this Libra's unique gifts. These are Libras looking for recognition and a place to be noticed for their abilities. They may be excellent presenters, interested in theater, or writing for school papers and journals. Whatever their niche is, they are looking to make a name in it, even if it just looks like landing on the honor roll. And beyond the classroom, these Libras look to find communities and extra curricular activities that keep their spirits high and value their bright energy. They're looking for teams and clubs that can recognize and utilize their talents.

Sun in Libra and Venus in Virgo:

With Venus in Virgo, these Libra students have high standards and exacting expectations. Studious at heart, these folks are looking to get things right and need to feel prepared. They are natural notetakers and are likely to be well read. And thanks to their wealth of knowledge, they test well, too, as they take in information rather technically and systematically. They may have an aptitude for math, science, or trade programs, or find that language is what calls to them most. Writing allows them to speak up in ways that they may be shy to voice aloud or off the cuff. These are also students that have a lot on their mind and may need specialized teachers or programs to best keep them on track. Mentoring and tutoring (both in giving and receiving such services) are likely to be helpful for these Libras, as they respond well to accountability and detailed instruction. Outside of the classroom, these students look for ways to quell excess nervous energy. Sometimes their release strategies look like staying in and playing it safe, and sometimes they just need a good distraction and mental escape. Regardless of their vices, it is important for these Libras to have clear schedules and regular routines in place around their schooling.

Sun in Libra and Venus in Libra:

Libra students with Venus in Libra are measured and easy, never working too hard. They aim to please, rarely making much of a fuss, except maybe for passing notes or chatting with their neighbor. These folks are social and engaged, and they love a good group project or partner assignment. They are also more likely to bond or meld to their teachers, learning early on of the benefits to be had from a supervisor in their favor. As for interests, these Libras lean in to the arts, literature, debate, and theory. They are attracted to elegant ideas and studies of correlation. In the classroom, they are well suited to discussion-based courses and learning that is conversational and engaging. Without enough interest, these students can be ambivalent about their studies and more invested in their relationships at school. Often social butterflies, these Libras are well connected and like to maintain a good image. Their desire for harmony and contentment makes them friendly and cool, making sure to maintain the good graces of any peer they meet.

Sun in Libra and Venus in Scorpio:

For the Venus in Scorpio, their Libra Sun maintains a little more focus and the ability to intensely commit. Depending on the topic, these Libras are just as capable of caring immensely as to giving zero interest at all. They can run toward extremes and have a stubborn streak when they don't like or agree with something. These are the Libras most likely to say no and to rebel when they feel challenged. But when they are on board, they're all in. This is a student that can tenaciously go after a goal and pour their heart into it, with their sharp intellect shining through. They can also find themselves in heated debates and may obsess over certain topics or subjects that call to them. Depending on their teachers, they can be dedicated students for mentors that recognize their acuity, but they may turn difficult if they don't feel appropriately respected. And similarly, they are likely to make close bonds with a small group of peers that value them for their magnetic and emotional depths.

Sun in Libra and Venus in Sagittarius:

Libras with Venus in Sagittarius see school as yet another place to explore. There is often an interest in history and epic stories for this Libra, as they are drawn to understanding the big-picture hows and whys of our world. Similarly, they are skilled at studying theology and philosophical topics, as those, too, examine greater truths. And for some, they see no better teacher than life itself, in which case they may not really be invested in institutions or traditional school at all. But when stuck in a classroom, they make sure to make it fun. These Libras may become a class clown or get restless when studies feel too stale and serious. It's ideal for them to find hands-on learning experiences and not to be stuck too long behind a desk. They may enjoy the freedom they find in PE or on an after-school team, where they can socialize and move around. And they're also likely candidates for a study abroad or cultural club, where they can build relationships with folks from different backgrounds.

LIBRA
in Daily Life

Daily life demands balance, discernment, and compromise, and luckily these are all guiding principles for the Libra lifestyle. They know how to structure their days for both pleasure and productivity, and they do it in good taste. From a distance, they appear to have it all and embody a fluid and effortless grace. But underneath this elegant vision, much effort is being made to keep their world an easy and even one.

The foundation of their day is likely to start with sleep. Their Venusian nature craves rest and restoration, needing tender time to renew. And the scales know inherently that being at rest is as valuable as being busy. A good night's sleep is paramount to a happy and healthy human, and for Libra there should be little compromises around this truth. In fact, there may be a more than "normal" need for this rest. As their season is that of the equinox, when the night reaches equilibrium to the day, their energy is of a similar pattern. Libras can often be in need of more than just a solid eight hours to fully recuperate and readily emerge into the next day.

Once they do emerge, however, their mornings can hold a similar sense of slowness or indulgence. Libras like to start their days with ease and have various morning vices. For some it's the snooze button, for others it may be a morning pastry, or perhaps a long shower or the news in bed. They're not ones to start the day in a stressful rush, as it's against their nature. So when they do have to be somewhere early, they're likely to plan ahead and have their morning laid out.

Mornings are also a time for to-do lists, as Libras need to know their priorities in order to keep a balanced schedule. It's likely, however, that lists will pop up throughout the day, as they're an easy way for Libras to process and discern what's on their plate at any given moment. Plus it doesn't hurt that crossing off a task is more than enough cause for rest or reward. Libras respond quite well to the right motivation and make sure that their days have enough sweet spots to keep them going.

Play and pause, for the most part, are woven throughout all that they do. In their need for life to both look and feel good, every day demands at least one small joy. They are driven to self-sustain their silver linings and share their delights with those who are near them. When life feels challenging, they keep it in perspective by remembering how soft things can be and cultivating a thoughtful calm. For some Libras, when faced with difficulties, comfort can most easily be found in the warm words of others, both in person and in writing. Reminders of how and why the human spirit triumphs and finds comfort can soothe the troubled Libra mind. Words, in general, give great meaning to their days.

Avid communicators, Libras need to feel that they are in touch on a daily basis. They are often readers and almost certainly wired into various social networks. Group chats, phone calls, social media, and the like can feel like lifelines for a Libra. These outlets help them stay connected to their relationships and also keep their minds and hearts engaged. They are hungry for human contact and information, and they like to be up to date on the latest threads and links amidst their world. And they don't mind the distraction it can provide either, especially when their day has yet to captivate or entertain them.

Real-world face time is equally as important. Libras give a lot of time to the people they love and often seek out opportunities to partner and work with others. Kids, clients, or suitors, Libras will shape their days around the needs of their most important bonds. They maintain a number of meaningful relationships that fill and guide their schedules, including their relationship with themselves. In order to best give to others, they need to feel centered within themselves, and they can do this in a number of ways.

The personal routines of Libra are often gentle and aesthetically oriented, emphasizing restorative care. Many are drawn to dance, yoga, or Pilates, body-based practices that are elegant and light but refined in their movements. Some may have a regular practice of journaling, as a place to reflect and clear their heads. Nearly all have a practice of beauty, extending from themselves far into their surroundings. Libras take regular care of their appearance and invest in things that bring out their own sense of style and allure. But beyond their own looks, they also strive to cultivate enchanting environments. Their homes, offices, and studios are a reflection of their taste and places that receive routine tending. Style is a part of all they do, as they are emboldened and fortified by grace made visible.

ADVANCED CONSIDERATIONS

Exploring the daily life of a Libra, there are many essential themes, but it's not the whole picture. To get a better idea of the idiosyncrasies of different Libras, we need to look to their Venus placement. In examining these placements, we can understand one's specific motivation.

VENUS PLACEMENTS

Sun in Libra and Venus in Leo:

Libras with Venus in Leo have a need for regular indulgence and a little "me time" in their daily routine. These Libras have big hearts and are very generous, but they also know that self-care is an equal priority. From this place, they manage to make the mundane more tolerable by sprinkling in fun treats throughout the day. Whether it looks like a lavish latte or lathering on luxurious products, these Libras invest in quality care that makes them feel good. They're able to endure their fair share and take on a lot for their loved ones, but not without these small moments in place. And beyond their creature comforts, these Libras need regular interaction with others. Opportunities to share in warmth and affection are paramount for these folks, so shared meals, coffee dates, or simple meetups with friends are non-negotiable needs.

Sun in Libra and Venus in Virgo:

For the Libra with Venus in Virgo, their days are task driven, as they are the masters of a to-do list. These Libras are planners and like to have an efficiency to their days. But that doesn't mean they always stick to their plans. They're often the first to volunteer their time or get roped into helping others out, and they can sometimes struggle with adequate self-care. When they're on their game, though, and able to equally prioritize their health and rest routines, they're as helpful and productive as can be. It is important that they are able to make time for their own physical care and that these Libras eat well, with balanced nutrition and gentle foods. While they are quite skilled at dropping everything to help a friend, they are less so at dealing with their own crises and can feel rattled when they can't get to all the details of their day.

Sun in Libra and Venus in Libra:

In daily life for Venus in Libra, the focus is on ease. These Libras are likely to have simple beauty routines and to enjoy leisurely mornings. Whether it's sleeping in, lingering with coffee, or reading the news over breakfast, comfort is key, and they don't like to rush. There is a need for the right pace throughout the day, and they focus on keeping a balanced schedule. These Libras are the masters of the work-life balance and beyond, knowing that they need just the right mix of time given to self, rest, engagement, and effort. They also know how to compromise in response to this need, as some days will lean a little heavier or lighter than others. With clear boundaries, though, these Libras live well and find ways to weave art, connection, and conversation throughout their days.

Sun in Libra and Venus in Scorpio:

As a Libra with Venus in Scorpio, their day is determined by passion and one's cravings. These Libras are dedicated to their work and responsibilities, but they also have clear boundaries for how much they'll give to whom and to what. Their days start with centering and engaging their personal power, which may look like meditation, a morning run, or just slipping into their power suit. Time with chosen family, loves, and friends is also very important and will be factored in throughout their days. But of all the Libras, these are the most likely to spend stretches of time alone. They may be the type to journal or reflect, or they may have their own vices to help them blow off steam. And as much as they are able to work hard, they balance their efforts by playing hard, too, when it's all said and done.

Sun in Libra and Venus in Sagittarius:

For Venus in Sagittarius, their daily routine is likely to fluctuate. These Libras need a sense of adventure in each day and can't be too caught up in longstanding routines. It all depends on their current interests, which could be meditative yoga one week and trail running the next. These folks need their lives to be rich with meaning, and they'll recalibrate each day to reach for whatever vision they're called to most. They're always keeping their eye out for new fun and pleasures they have yet to try, and they may take classes or join meetups throughout their week. These Libras strive to keep their days enlivening and make regular time to connect with friends, sharing stories, jokes, and joy.

RISING SIGNS

In addition to the Venus placement for a Libra, daily lives are astrologically influenced by a number of factors. So to better understand the day-to-day style of different Libras, we're going to explore the influence of their rising signs. This layer is yet another detail that coexists with the character as described previously by their Venus signs.

Aries Rising and Sun in Libra:

For the Libra with Aries rising, their daily life requires a clear balance between self and others. They're natural go-getters, but they feel most themselves when partnering with people. These folks are also sure to need plenty of quality rest to take on their days and are intentional with their time and commitments.

Taurus Rising and Sun in Libra:

With Taurus rising, the Libra Sun has a real need for routines and a focus on their health. These Libras need a structured schedule, balanced diet, and regular self-care. They are also likely to work in some service capacity and are the masters of completing tasks and running errands.

Gemini Rising and Sun in Libra:

Libras with Gemini rising have a need for daily creative expression. They are full of ideas and inherently social, needing lots of opportunities for communication and play. These Libras have a healthy sense of humor and may be drawn to childcare or thrive as fun parents.

Cancer Rising and Sun in Libra:

As a Cancer rising Libra, the routine is likely to revolve in and around the home or family. These Libras need regular rest and reprieve, prioritizing safety and familiarity in their days. They are also rather sensitive folks that long for simple pleasures and a well-kept nest. Their daily routine is likely to shift with their emotions and to be comfort driven.

Leo Rising and Sun in Libra:

With Leo rising, the Libra routine is tied to their community and local scene. These folks take pleasure in their neighborhood and are often the keepers of the social web. They're constant communicators, with days filled by texts, emails, coffee dates, and calls. Everyday errands are tackled with ease and keep them connected to their crew.

Virgo Rising and Sun in Libra:

For the Virgo rising Libra, daily life is centered around values and resources. These Libras are focused on making shrewd investments of their time and are frequently evaluating their commitments. Their routines are often measured, cautious, and carefully calculated to be as efficient and impactful as possible with their limited energy.

Libra Rising and Sun in Libra:

As Libras with Libra rising, their days are rather self-directed and centered around making connections. They are likely to have some sort of daily beauty routine and to enjoy a leisurely pace in their days, modeling balance and grace in

their chosen lifestyle. And there is a notable need for socializing and bonding with others on an everyday basis.

Scorpio Rising and Sun in Libra:
With Scorpio rising, Libras have a greater need for rest and
pause in their days. These Libras may be drawn to devo-
tional or meditative practices and require windows of calm
and still to reset themselves. While still needing to regularly
engage, for these folks connection is often found in holding
space for life's difficulties and unspoken truths with others.

Sagittarius Rising and Sun in Libra:
For the Libra with Sagittarius rising, their days see them
swept up in groups or on committees. These folks are regularly engaged in their communities and prioritize activism
in their daily life. They spend frequent time with friends and
like to have plenty of space to vision and share their dreams.

Capricorn Rising and Sun in Libra:
Libras with Capricorn rising are often of great service to
the public and spend much of their time out working in

the world. These Libras are visible connectors and dedicate much of their time to their chosen career and calling. They're serious and responsible, with clear boundaries around their time and commitments.

Aquarius Rising and Sun in Libra:

With Aquarius rising, the Libra Sun is in pursuit of ideas and experiences. These Libras have a very airy nature and like to talk about big ideas or strike up conversations with strangers. They are likely to prioritize continued study and opportunities to travel whenever possible. In their day to day, they need regular connection to new people, places, and perspectives.

Pisces Rising and Sun in Libra:

For the Libra with Pisces rising, their days are of a slower and more reclusive manner. Often the managers of shared resources, both tangible and intangible, these Libras spend a good deal of time wrapped up in the stickier bits of other people's lives. And when not examining the hidden depths of others, they crave rest and intimacy with close partners.

8

LIBRA

in the World

Zooming out to see the big picture, Libras hold a special place in the world. And similarly, they hold a special place in the zodiac, as each of the signs do. So to get a sense of Libra's larger purpose, it helps to look into how they fit in with the rest of the signs.

In just looking at zodiacal order, they are the seventh sign, sitting right in the middle of it all. This reminds us of how they are the point of equilibrium, markers of the exchange from one side to another. And so they are. Libras serve as intermediaries in the world, helping to keep us all connected. They hold the balance and maintain our relationships. Vital to our networks, they sustain our lines of communication not only through their positioning, but also through the element of air.

As air signs in the world, they are responsible for sharing ideas. The air element is tied to language, conversation, the mind, breath, and expression. It is shared and life sustaining. And the signs of this element share in its gifts. Whereas earth signs are well grounded and water signs are intuitive, the air signs are endowed with the gift of logic. They are the thinkers and employ reason to make sense of their surroundings and experiences. Along with Gemini and Aquarius, Libra is in the world to demonstrate the gift of thought, of an open and airy mind. Often these signs stick together, as their shared element allows for shared understanding and a similar temperament. They also pair comfortably with the fire signs—Aries, Leo, and Sagittarius—as their elements share an uplifting effect, and they easily entertain and inspire one another.

Another layer to Libra's place in the world is their cardinal sensibility. Libras bring with them the gift of initiation and share this fluency with their fellow cardinal signs Aries, Cancer, and Capricorn. Each of these signs is tasked with bringing and beginning something new in the world. They are the folks that bring forth sudden changes and fresh starts. For the Libra, they are here to help us forge new relationships. Libras initiate connections, draw boundaries, and create art. They help us to form new ideas about who we are and how we are held together.

And more than just starting relationships, Libras are

here to bond us in the name of Venus. As a sign of Venus, along with Taurus, they demonstrate what it means to be in connection with pleasure and with heart. Both of these signs have a great deal to teach the world about love and joy, and they do so in very different manners. Libra is responsible for linking our hearts to our minds. They connect through air and seek to exchange and express the gifts of Venus whereas their fellow Venusian, Taurus, takes care of connecting our hearts to our bodies. Bearing their specific sweetness, Libra looks to make the world a more comfortable and inviting place through social relationships and ideals of elegance and grace.

One other relationship worth noting for Libra is their connection to the sign of Aries. Libra opposes Aries, and this dynamic acts as a very important influence for both of them. In their opposition, they are inherently tied, facing one another from two different sides. It can appear as though they are exclusively at odds, but really, they are on a shared spectrum. While it is easy to paint Aries as feisty and independent, with Libra sitting as pliant and accommodating, these are also traits they can learn from each other and share. In their opposition, they reflect upon one another, illuminating the links between them. From this relationship, Libra learns how to prioritize both self and other in the world because they can see how the two natures are inseparable.

Exploring these facets of Libra's connections to the zodiac helps to elucidate their place in the world, as mirrored by their place amongst the other signs. Libras carry a distinct and invaluable energy for the collective, and their roles here are versatile and many. No matter what their title or status, most are in pursuit of ideals, holding out hope for a better world and working to incite change. They are minds seeking harmony and understanding. They are advocates for humanity and for peace. As you will soon see, so many Libras are acclaimed writers, philosophers, and thinkers. And even when in positions of glamor and ease, they are still often activists and ambassadors of justice in the world.

ADVANCED CONSIDERATIONS

As we've been examining the effects of Venus for Libra throughout this book, it's now time to look at some real-world examples. The following is a collection of well-known Libras that have been organized and grouped by their Venus placements. In comparing these groups, we begin to see how Venus influences the embodiment of the Libra Sun in the lives of others.

VENUS PLACEMENTS

Sun in Libra and Venus in Leo:

With Venus in Leo, Libras are meant to share their light and vitality with the world. They are performers, entertainers, and have big, vibrant hearts with much to share. Famed burlesque dancer and entrepreneur Dita Von Teese is an excellent example of this placement. She is known for her signature style and enticing others to indulge in her glamorous world of pleasure. Fellow Venus in Leo performer Donald Glover is a creative well known for his music, acting, and writing. He is a multitalented performer who exudes charisma, creativity, and warmth. Truman Capote shared this placement as well and was an influential writer with a penchant for drama and celebrity. Other famous Libras with this placement include actor Tessa Thompson, actor Olivia Newton-John, musician James Blake, rapper T.I., broadcast journalist Barbara Walters, fashion designer Donna Karan, and rapper A$AP Rocky.

Sun in Libra and Venus in Virgo:

Libras with Venus in Virgo fill the world with glorious details and sincere service. They provide humanity with meaningful information and are compassionately critical. Acclaimed musician St. Vincent is a shining example of the exquisite intricacies this combo can create, as her music is masterfully nuanced and finessed, both in its sound and in her performance and presentation. Painter Mark Rothko is another Libra with Venus in Virgo, and his famed color-field works reflect this Libra's appreciation for details, subtlety, and simplicity as most impactful. Hasan Minhaj, a comedian and political commentator, demonstrates this placement's gift for language and discernment and is a voice for the decency this style of Libra wishes for the world. Other famous Libras with this placement include musician John Coltrane, actor Julie Andrews, philosopher Friedrich Nietzsche, filmmaker

Guillermo del Toro, singer Toni Braxton, fashion editor Diana Vreeland, and model Amber Rose.

Sun in Libra and Venus in Libra:

For Libras with Venus in Libra, their aim in the world is to incite harmony and compassion. These Libras are looking for justice, connection, pleasure, and ease, and they are looking to share. Writer and activists bell hooks truly carries this spirit of Libra energy, as her work is centered around equality and love that is tender, inclusive, and just. TV's favorite judge and arbiter of the law Judge Judy also has Venus in Libra, and she is often the literal embodiment of the Justice card that symbolizes a Libra. Also carrying this placement is Will Smith, the well-known actor and celebrity, who is generally seen to be very charming and affable both on and off screen. Other famous Libras with this placement include cellist Yo-Yo Ma, filmmaker Spike Jonze, actor and dancer Rita Hayworth, writer Oscar Wilde, philosopher Michel Foucault, writer Roxane Gay, and musician Natalie Maines.

Sun in Libra and Venus in Scorpio:

The Libras with Venus in Scorpio come into the world with something to prove, with passion and a bit of bite. They look for complexity and depth in the world, and they know how to find sweetness where others are too afraid to look. Serena Williams, the world-renowned tennis player and mogul, demonstrates the focus and intensity that this placement can bring. She models fierce kindness, elegant strength, and total agility both on and off the court. Esoteric writer and teacher Mary K. Greer is also a Libra with Venus in Scorpio, and she has dedicated much work to making the mystical tool of the tarot accessible and healing for many. In another realm of taboo and mind-expanding study, the Venus in Scorpio psychologist Timothy Leary focused his work on the effects of psychedelics in a therapeutic capacity, looking for aid in the illicit. Other famous Libras with this placement include rapper MC Lyte, musician Thelonius Monk, actor Fran Drescher, rapper Cardi B, actor Brie Larson, peace activist Mahatma Gandhi, and musician Bruce Springsteen.

Sun in Libra and Venus in Sagittarius:

With Venus in Sagittarius, Libra sees the world as a place to explore and share inspiration. They take on the world with great faith, with bold enthusiasm, and in pursuit of higher meaning at every turn. Entertainer and stunt performer Evel Knievel embodied the energy fully, choosing a life of thrills, entertaining the world with his motorcycle jumps. Activist and politician Alexandria Ocasio-Cortez carries a fearlessness to lead, trailblazing as the youngest woman to serve in U.S. Congress. Actor Jeff Goldblum is another prime example of this placement, as he is widely adored for his charming, offbeat, and spirited nature. Other famous Libras with this placement includes fashion editor André Leon Talley, musician and performer Nico, musician Paul Simon, New Age writer Deepak Chopra, film star Lillian Gish, musician Dizzy Gillespie, and actor Suzanne Somers.

RISING SIGNS

In addition to Venus placements, it's time to look at how the rising sign influences Libras in a real-world context. The list below names various Libras for each of the 12 rising signs and presents living examples of this energy at work. Their Venus placements have also been included, so that we can note how these layers merge and coexist, serving to further inform the Libra personality.

Aries Rising and Sun in Libra:

For the Libra Suns with Aries rising, their work in the world involves taking action and holding space for others' experience. They are connectors and go-getters, models of integrity, and able to shift from leader to listener with ease. Famous Libras with this placement include actor Brie Larson (Venus in Scorpio), comedian Janeane Garofalo (Venus in Leo), astrologer Stephen Arroyo (Venus in Scorpio), and actor Heather Locklear (Venus in Virgo).

Taurus Rising and Sun in Libra:

Libras with Taurus rising are tasked to show up in the world as stable and well rounded. Their impact is often made in the realms of health and wellness, and they can be seen as visionaries, with thoughtful analyses and critiques. Famous Libras with this placement include rapper Snoop

Dogg (Venus in Scorpio), actor Sigourney Weaver (Venus in Scorpio), athlete Serena Williams (Venus in Scorpio), and writer Ursula K. Le Guin (Venus in Libra).

Gemini Rising and Sun in Libra:

With Gemini rising, Libras are most interested in sharing their creative gifts with the world. These Libras are witty, insightful, playful, and expressive. They have a marked interest in children and artistic projects, looking to see joy and life prioritized and celebrated. Famous Libras with this placement include writer bell hooks (Venus in Libra), musician Thelonius Monk (Venus in Scorpio), musician Bruce Springsteen (Venus in Scorpio), and actor Nick Cannon (Venus in Virgo).

Cancer Rising and Sun in Libra:

As Cancer rising Libras, their worldly work is tied to their legacy, family, and roots. They are quite sensitive and intuitive, and they use these skills to build foundations of beauty and calm, as well as safe nests. These Libras can seem a little shy, but they are here to model the power and grace of vulnerability. Famous Libras with this placement include fashion editor Diana Vreeland (Venus in Virgo), singer Keyshia Cole (Venus in Sagittarius), writer William Faulkner (Venus in Leo), and supermodel Cheryl Tiegs (Venus in Libra).

Leo Rising and Sun in Libra:

With Leo rising, Libras keep the world connected and engaged. They are able to entertain the masses with their sparkling and accessible personalities. Their eager curiosity and enjoyment of life is contagious and keeps our days bright. Famous Libras with this placement include actor Angela Lansbury (Venus in Sagittarius), actor Roger Moore (Venus in Virgo), musician Sting (Venus in Virgo), and singer Gal Costa (Venus in Virgo).

Virgo Rising and Sun in Libra:

Libras with Virgo rising come into this world modeling lived values and a polite grace. They are humble yet bubbly figures, and they are committed to quality in all that they do.

These Libras make great teachers and are earnest in their work and chosen field. Famous Libras with this placement include actor Marion Cotillard (Venus in Leo), actor and musician Donald Glover (Venus in Leo), musician Paul Simon (Venus in Sagittarius), and television personality Kelly Ripa (Venus in Scorpio).

Libra Rising and Sun in Libra:

The Libra rising Libra speaks to the world from a place of experience. They are the embodiment of balance, justice, and tact, and their style exudes these truths. They're well spoken, with eloquent ideas to share with the world. And they're as charming as they are sweet. Famous Libras with this placement include writer Roxane Gay (Venus in Libra), writer T. S. Eliot (Venus in Libra), writer Arthur Rimbaud (Venus in Libra), and chef Emeril Lagasse (Venus in Virgo).

Scorpio Rising and Sun in Libra:

With Scorpio rising, a Libra is asked to work in the world's hidden and unseen realms. They are here to make sense of suffering, make friends with the downtrodden, and make peace with release and surrender. These Libras have an air of intensity and often exist in more spiritual or behind-the-scenes roles. Famous Libras with this placement include esoteric writer Mary K. Greer (Venus in Scorpio), philosopher Michel Foucault (Venus in Libra), actor Naomi Watts (Venus in Scorpio), and musician Bryan Ferry (Venus in Virgo).

Sagittarius Rising and Sun in Libra:

The Libras with Sagittarius rising in the world are here to experience and connect with a wild abandon. They can be the visionaries or the socially beloved, and they are very tied into the hive mind. These Libras want to imbue the world with more meaning and share their ideals of tolerance and peace. Famous Libras with this placement include singer Johnny Mathis (Venus in Virgo), psychologist Timothy Leary (Venus in Scorpio), musician Marc Bolan (Venus in Libra), and celebrity Kim Kardashian (Venus in Virgo).

Capricorn Rising and Sun in Libra:

Libras with Capricorn rising are the role models of the world. They are here to serve as examples of kindness, beauty, and charisma in action. They are the diplomats, the serious artists, representatives of integrity and justice. These Libras are cool and discerning, wanting to see the world a more composed place. Famous Libras with this placement include actor Carrie Fisher (Venus in Virgo), actor Zac Efron (Venus in Scorpio), singer Ashanti (Venus in Virgo), and musician Ed Droste (Venus in Scorpio).

Aquarius Rising and Sun in Libra:

As Libras with Aquarius rising, their role in the world is to captivate others with their ideas. They are big thinkers and philosophers, looking to find higher meaning and purpose in the world. These Libras are here to experience new things and make connections across perceived boundaries. Famous Libras with this placement include actor Alicia Silverstone (Venus in Scorpio), writer F. Scott Fitzgerald (Venus in Libra), stunt performer Evel Knievel (Venus in Sagittarius), and musician Jerry Lee Lewis (Venus in Virgo).

Pisces Rising and Sun in Libra:

Libras with Pisces rising are here to explore the hidden worlds of other people. They are often pulled into psychology or esoteric study, and they can also be wrapped up in the resources (financial or otherwise) of other people. Their temperament is dreamy and sensitive, so they are able to slip into the realms of shadow and psyche. Famous Libras with this placement include musician John Coltrane (Venus in Virgo), writer Deepak Chopra (Venus in Sagittarius), actor Gwyneth Paltrow (Venus in Leo), and actor Jason Alexander (Venus in Leo).

CONCLUSION

Having run the gamut from childhood to world renown, we've come to know a thing or two about Libra. The details of each life phase have been laid out and picked apart, including their likes and the dislikes, and all the stuff in between. Plenty of information has been shared to paint a lively portrait of the sign. And yet, no matter the nuance, the essence of Libra still remains simple and true. As stated at the beginning, Libras are the sign of the scales, they are of Venus, and they are cardinal and air.

While much can be said about Libra, these basics can tell you all that you really need to know. They are the bare bones of the Libra resolve. They are what inform a Libra's nature in any circumstance. They are how we know that Libras are balanced, charming, inviting, and bright. Libras are the ones to remind us of our sacred bonds and our ties to each other—of what meaningful relationships can help us become.

And every Libra has their own way. Venus has different directives for different Libras. Some are asked to partner with fairness, while others are asked to make peace with a little more grit. Those born at one hour may grow up timid and quiet, while those of another may be more outspoken and wild. There is a full and rich spectrum of Libras in the world, shaped by many different factors, both known and unknown. And there is also the factor of free will.

No matter the Libra, they have agency and they have say in who they become. What they do with their gifts and their fears and their hopes is entirely up to them. The Libra Sun imbues them with certain potentials and lights in them certain curiosities, but what they choose to do with this disposition is open ended. It is something they get to explore and engage in throughout their journey, that they will eventually come to know and embody in a singular way.

The astrology of Libra is a living, breathing thing. And it is an energy that longs to see us together, and to see us striving for justice. So Libra Sun or not, know that the sign of the scales is a facet within all of us and that we are all heartened to share in its ease and love.

INDEX

ABOUT THE AUTHOR

Gabrielle Moritz is an astrologer and creative currently based in the Pacific Northwest. She has been studying the stars now for a decade, and currently runs her astrology and design practice as Decent Astro. Her style of astrology is a blend of traditional and modern techniques translated through a compassionate and intuitive lens. Gabrielle is most interested in utilizing astrology to illuminate and uncover our true nature and to improve our ability to meaningfully understand and collaborate with time. She would love for you to learn more than just your Sun sign.

To follow more of her work or get in touch,
visit www.decentastro.com.

OTHER BOOKS IN THIS SERIES

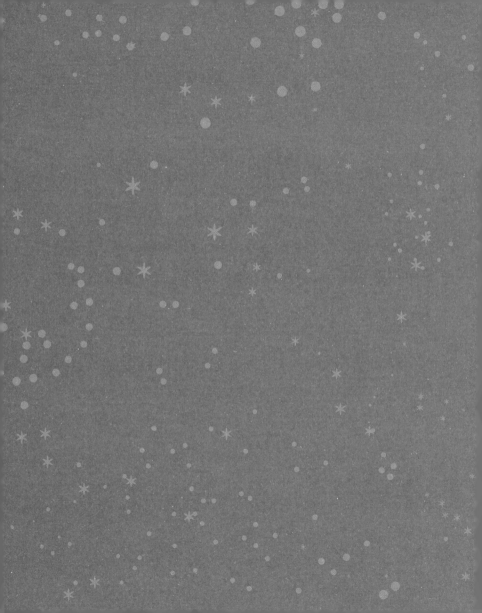